MORE THAN JUST A NAME
A Story about the Call Field Memorial Monument

by
Kenny Mayo

The Production of this Book was Sponsored by:
Museum of North Texas History
North Texas Genealogical Association
Wichita County Archives
Medrith Collins
Paul & Jennifer Fleming
Byrle & JoAnn Graham
Robert Kadane
Robert & Jeanie Seabury
Michael & Karen Smith

Cover Design by John Yates
Book Design by Peggy Browning
Edited by Becky Tuck

More Books by Kenny Mayo
Honky Tonk Heroes
Would You Like Mayo With That?
I'm Not a Preacher, But If I Was…This is What I Would Say

Through a combined effort at the Museum of North Texas History, the North Texas Genealogical Association, and the Wichita County Archives, an attempt has been made to call attention to the sacrifice made by Americans to the World War I effort at Call Field. This book is dedicated to the ever-present thread that has connected this area to the military branches of our government. From the first remote frontier forts to Call Field to present day Sheppard Air Force Base, the connection has remained an integral part of our city and area history.

Thanks to the researchers at the Wichita Falls Genealogical Association headed by President Joan Gray, Bryce Blair, county archivist, Becky Tuck, and Peggy Browning, book designer.

North Texas Genealogy Association Call Field Researchers:
Seated L to R: Joyce Gilleland, Sandy Person, Debbie Nelson
Standing L to R: Marilyn Meador, Mike Moody, Ed Ball, Jimmy Russell, Cheri Rix
Not Pictured: Eyvonne Rogers, Joan Gray

MORE THAN JUST A NAME

E.M. Anderson

E.B. Arnold

E. B. Babcock

B.G. Beach

C.A. Chiles

F. D. Cryer

J.R. DesChamps

R.F. Farren

O.G. Franks

H.P Game

G.C. Hail

C. E. Holburn

Harold Imbrie

J. B. Jackson, Jr.

T. H. James

W. H. Lees

A.K. Lincoln

W. McBride

F.R. McGriffin

O. A. Petriet

E. V. Rhodes

H. S. Ross

C.L. Stevens

H. H. Thomas

J. T. Van Auken

S. R. Warner

P.T. Whittle

C. Williams

They did not come here to die; that was not in their plans. They were just coming to a remote military post named Call Field in the north central Texas town of Wichita Falls. Each had joined the war effort for his own reason. Some were driven by honor, some by duty, others for adventure, and some to get a better chance at life; but whatever the reason, all would see their lives end here in this place.

To understand why they came here, you must understand the events that preceded their arrival. World War I had been going on for 32 months in Europe, and the United States, led by President Woodrow Wilson, had managed to stay out of the fighting.

Tensions periodically escalated between the U.S. and Germany, first in 1915 with the sinking of the Lusitania by German U-Boats, killing 1,200 people, and 128 of them Americans.

Then, the Zimmerman Telegraph was discovered in January of 1917, in which Germany promised Mexico the restoration of her lands in America in return for Mexico's help in the war.

Following Wilson's reelection, public support for involvement in the war swelled and pushed him to declare war on Germany on April 6, 1917, with the United States entering on the Allied side in a war that was supposed to "end all wars."

Aerial View of Call Field

The next few pages are taken in large part from an article written by Dr. Dwight Tuttle, historian at Sheppard Air Force Base for the 1991 publication, Wichita Heritage.

"In response to that declaration of war, Frank Kell and Joseph A. Kemp, the two most influential citizens in Wichita Falls, assisted by other townspeople, began a 3-month campaign to persuade the War Department to bring one of its newest military weapons, the aeroplane, and the accompanying aviation training field here. If successful, it would make Wichita Falls one of 32 training fields for aviation in the United States. A meeting called by Kemp on May 21, 1917 raised $35,000 to obtain a site for the training camp. Kemp and Kell privately donated $20,000. In addition, Kemp told the Chamber of Commerce he would stand behind the proposal for $64,000.

On June 16, 1917, the Southern Aviation Department in San Antonio chose Wichita Falls as the site for an air-training field. The name of the field would be Call Field, named after1st Lt. Loren Call, who had died in a plane crash on July 9, 1913 in Texas City, Texas.

After the announcement, the City of Wichita Falls began preparations for the location of the field by filling two small ponds on the grounds and cutting trees and fences. The field was a boon to the economy of the area, providing money and jobs to a growing city.

F. N. Lawton, a member of the Chamber of Commerce, noted that the pipes were all ordered and rushed through on government service. Between 2,500 and 3,000 men worked to build the airfield. Every available team of horses in the area hauled materials that included millions of feet of lumber.

Utility lines, including water and electricity, were extended to the field and paid for by the City of Wichita Falls. City officials persuaded the Missouri-Texas-Kansas Railroad to lay track to Call Field at no cost to the city.

By November 18, 1917, Major George Krapt, the acting commandant, reported that the field was 95% complete. By the middle of the month, officers began arriving at the post, followed soon by aviators and signal corps personnel.

Three squadrons, the 164th, the 165th, and the 198th arrived in December; and the stage was set for the start-up of training aviators for the war effort.

At its prime, Call Field had 55 buildings. The complex consisted of 12 hangars, a hospital, 6 mess halls, an officers' club, a bakery, and other support facilities.

Call Field Hospital

Robert Seabury, noted land developer in this area and a historian of Call Field, said that the perimeters of the field in present day (2019) terms would be the curve on Call Field Road by the Realtors Association Building (that was the main gate), then went as far west as Fairway Boulevard. North to south boundaries would have been north by Kell Boulevard and south to about midway to Southwest Parkway.

By March of 1918, officials had developed a well-rounded curriculum consisting of ground gunnery, aerial gunnery, radio, theoretical flying, practical flying, airplanes, and motors. It also included army paperwork, guard manual, close order drill; and calisthenics, photography, reconnaissance, aerial liaison, and miniature observation.

Aerial Photo School at Call Field

Pilots trained on both the Curtiss-Jenny and Standard biplanes. The Curtiss-Jenny was powered by a Hall Scott engine and was capable of flying 75-100 miles per hour. However, it would not run for any length of time and was unreliable in cold weather. The Standard biplane was more reliable but was clumsy and slow and was controlled entirely by the rudder.

Pilots could take off from one of two dirt runways, one or both, filled with prairie dog holes. They would fly over Lake Wichita and then continue in flight for 60 to 75 miles, or an hour and a half, whichever came first. Several area communities had designated fields where the pilots could land. Pilots were regarded as colorful figures, and many towns competed for playing host to them on cross-country flights.

Runway at Call Field

Insight into these men who became pilots reveals the typical mentality of young men, aged 20 and slightly older, from whatever century you select them. They are ten feet tall and bullet proof, then or now.

A letter written back home to a Mansfield, Ohio newspaper by a young cadet named Roy "Mud" Gardner and discovered by a researcher, takes us inside their thoughts.

"At last I am at a real American aviation field where there are lots of aeroplanes and instructors. After graduating at Columbus from Ground School, I was sent out to Garden City, N.Y. to go 'overseas' for training, but before our bunch was sent, the government found they had too many cadets 'over there,' so we were sent to the different schools in Texas for training, and I landed here. (Call Field)

I have been here since Jan. 2 and was given my first flight the following morning. The first flight is mostly a joy-ride and to test you out. The instructor assigned to me pointed out to me a Curtiss J.N. 4 and told me to get in the rear seat, which I did, and fastened the safety belt around my waist. Then he got in the front seat, and after testing the motor the mechanic removed the blocks, and my instructor opened the throttle wide open, and the machine started along the earth.

You leave the ground so lightly and fast that you hardly realize you are off until about 50 feet up. The first flight lasted for 52 minutes. We went up until the altimeter read 5,200 feet. The earth by now was far below, and houses looked like cigar boxes and telegraph poles like toothpicks. A small stream looked like a long, thin snake; and well, everything looked so different.

Just as I was enjoying the scenery, the instructor gave me the controls, and I was busy for some time when he shook them, which was a sign for me to let loose. Just as I did the motor stopped, and we nosed over and started a straight dive for the earth.

I could look straight ahead and see the earth coming up at an awful clip. My heart came up to my mouth, and I could have bit it in two.

I didn't know whether the motor had stopped or if we were falling or what. We dropped a little over 1,000 feet and then the motor started, and he leveled her off. Then I realized he was trying to scare me, so I figured as soon as it was level, he would give me the controls to see if I was nervous. So, I got ready and sure enough he gave them to me, and I took hold and away we went.

After the first trip of 52 minutes, I sure was glad to get on the ground because then I did not have any too much faith in that bunch of wood, wire, and fabric. But after that I soon gained confidence, and in nice weather I now get about one hour each day in the air.

After four hours and 52 minutes of instruction, my instructor stepped out and told me to go alone, and I sure was glad for he is a very conservative fellow afraid that you will 'spill the beans' for him, and he told me one day when I wanted him to do stunts for me that I forgot he has a wife and family; so I now have been flying alone for a week and am learning much faster alone, for you know when you get in a bad place, it is up to you to get busy and get out."

Another pilot, F.E. Bingham's letter to his parents appeared in the Altoona Times in Altoona, Pennsylvania.

"It was a grand and glorious feeling when the wind pressed against my cheeks and nostrils, and I knew I was flying. I lost all interest in the ground and exulted in the ship which rode the air smoothly, more like a canoe than anything else. It was fascinating, but for the life of me, I felt no thrill. I couldn't convince myself there was any danger. When I looked over the cowl again the ground was 8,000 feet below, and I thought that the thrills of airplane riding had been overdrawn."

Like the other pilot's account, the plane went into a nosedive, and he mentions the wind howling and screeching in the bracing cables as the ground seemed to grow ever closer. They too pulled out of the dive, and he ended the letter with, *"but we landed safely after all."*

One example of this cavalier approach to life was in the Daily Arkansas Gazette from Little Rock, Arkansas dated April 18, 1918. The heading was:

KILL COYOTES FROM AIR – AVIATORS AT CALL FIELD INTRODUCE A NEW STUNT, Wichita Falls, Texas, April 17 ---. *"Civilian instructor Harmon Norton with a Call Field Cadet chased two coyotes in a field near Lake Wichita in their airplane last night and killed one animal by dipping to earth and striking it with a landing wheel. The hide, as evidence, is being dried at the cantonment today.*

The coyotes, probably believing the plane to be some new bird, attempted to keep pace with it as it glided along the earth. Instructor Norton dipped, thinking the animals would be frightened, but one stood its ground and offered fight. A second dip, well judged, killed the coyote."

Call Field commander at Lake Wichita Pavilion

"For the most part, citizens and soldiers co-existed in a cordial relationship. The home of Joseph Kemp located at 10th Street and Grant became sort of an informal USO for those serving at Call Field. Streetcars timed their rounds from the city to Lake Wichita to make sure they picked up soldiers at Call Field, so they could attend the dances held at the Lake Pavilion

Two major problems did exist from nearly the beginning and persisted until nearly the closing of the post. One was the water supply. 1917-1918 were horrible drought years for the Wichita Falls area, and originally the post had requested 50,000 gallons of water, which the Chamber of Commerce saw was provided.

However, as the field grew, so did demand, and the sanitary inspector for the Army threatened to shut down the post unless 100,000 gallons of water could be provided. Major Brooks upped that number to 125,000, but somehow that supply was met."[2]

The other issue was actually a combination of two problems that existed within military posts since the cavalry posts and accompanying Indian Wars. One was the abundance of alcohol. During its beginning, the nickname "Whiskeytaw Falls" was pinned on the city because of its ready availability of liquor.

Wichita Falls was a hot spot for not only troops here, but also at Fort Sill in Lawton, Oklahoma. Now with two military posts, Call Field on the outskirts of town and Fort Sill accessible by train, added to the already thirsty town folks, the question of how to control the abuse was presented.

Congress resolved the problem by passing a law in 1918, which forbade the sale of liquor within ten miles of a military installation. The legislation, known as the Volstead Act, served to limit the resource to some degree. Twenty-seven saloons closed their doors in Wichita Falls.

"The other problem which went along with the first was the presence of red-light districts, flourishing from an abundance of lonely men on one hand and a supply of 'working girls' on the other. In May 1918, Washington sent letters to city leaders here questioning their patriotism for allowing six houses of ill repute to not only exist but also flourish. It probably did not help anything that the director of Social Services at Call Field was arrested and convicted for violating the Mann Act.

The situation was finally resolved when the city and county officials in a joint resolution, decided that they would quarantine all suspicious women in town who showed signs of venereal disease. Soldiers at Call Field received orders that they could be court-martialed for consorting with such ladies, and eventually the problem subsided to some degree."[3]

So, this was the situation in 1918 when young men began arriving. They were businessmen, teachers, college students, and even one ex-hockey player. They came here to the fledging military post for whatever reason each had put together for their action, stepped onto the red dirt field and began their journey toward the final days of their lives.

This book is meant to chronicle that movement, particularly those last days which resulted in their deaths and their names inscribed on a monument to honor for ages the contribution they made.

Call Field's Mascot: A Raccoon Called Nic-O-Demus

FEBRUARY

The first casualty was 26-year-old Hubert Palmer Game. He was the son of Mateo Francisco Game, who had been born in Ecuador and Clara Game, born in Louisiana. He was a graduate of Cogswell College and the University Farm School at Davis, California. He had attended aviation school in California, graduating from there in December of 1917. He had been a salesman for the Union Fish Company in San Francisco, a large company that was a leader in the fish industry.

Hubert had signed up for the draft on June 5, 1917. He is listed as being of medium height with gray eyes and brown hair.

HUBERT PALMER GAME

Born in San Francisco, California, March 13, 1892

Attended Cogswell Polytechnic College, San Francisco
for two years

Enrolled in the University Farm School, Davis
September 1912

Charter Member, Phi Alpha Iota, (Sigma Alpha
Epsilon) Fraternity

Completed the two year course

Hubert Game

On February 8, 1918, Game was killed in a plane crash at Call Field when his plane fell several hundred feet to the ground. In the obituary that appeared in the Oakland newspaper, it mentions the fact that a detachment of infantry and twenty cadets from the aviation school there acted as a military escort for his service. Hubert Palmer Game was the first of many to die that year, 1918, at Call Field, far from the bay area of California and his family.

MILITARY FUNERAL FOR YOUNG AVIATOR

Funeral services for Hubert Palmer Game, young aviator who was killed in Texas last week, were conducted yesterday afternoon at 2210 Webster street. The services were conducted by Rev. Edgar F. Gee and Rev. F. W. Clampett, whose son was a college chum of Game.

A detachment of infantry from the Presidio and twenty cadets from the aviation school on the campus acted as military escort. Game was a graduate of Cogswell college and the University Farm school at Davis. He attended the aviation school on the campus, making a fine record according to the instructors and graduated here early in December. He was killed last Thursday when his machine fell several hundred feet to the ground.

Hubert Game Obituary

PLACE OF DEATH

TEXAS STATE BOARD OF HEALTH
Bureau of Vital Statistics

STANDARD CERTIFICATE OF DEATH

Reg. No. 1002

County Wichita

City Wichita Falls (No.) Call Field St.; Ward) (If death occurred in a hospital or institution, give its NAME instead of street and number)

FULL NAME Hubert P. Game

PERSONAL AND STATISTICAL PARTICULARS	MEDICAL PARTICULARS

SEX male   Color or Race white   Single, Married, Widowed, or Divorced (Write the word) Single

DATE OF DEATH Feb 8 1918

DATE OF BIRTH March 13 '92

I HEREBY CERTIFY, That I attended deceased from ___ 191__, to ___ 191__

AGE 25 yrs 10 mos 25 d

that I last saw h__ alive on ___ 191__,

and that death occurred, on the date stated above, at 8:00 A.m.

The CAUSE OF DEATH was as follows:

Fracture of skull, crushed body; Accidental death

OCCUPATION
(a) Trade, profession, or particular kind of work Flying Cadet
(b) General nature of industry, business, or establishment in which employed (or employer) at Call Field.

BIRTHPLACE (State or country) San Francisco, Cal.

Contributory (Secondary)

NAME OF FATHER

(Signed) Curtis Atkinson Capt. M.R.C.
Feb 8 18 (Address) Call Field Wichita Falls Texas

BIRTHPLACE OF FATHER (State or country) Unknown

MAIDEN NAME OF MOTHER Unknown

BIRTHPLACE OF MOTHER (State or country) Unknown

LENGTH OF RESIDENCE (For Hospitals, Institutions, Transients, or Recent Residents)

THE ABOVE IS TRUE TO THE BEST OF MY KNOWLEDGE

(Informant) Galen S. Horner
C.A.S.

(Address)

PLACE OF BURIAL OR REMOVAL   DATE OF BURIAL
Oakland, Cal.   191__

UNDERTAKER   ADDRESS

Hubert Game Death Certificate

22

The second casualty for the field came a few days later on February 10th. Thomas H.

James had been born in Chicago, Illinois in 1899 to Corvell and Ella James. Corvell was listed

as a fencing materials salesman in the 1910 census in which by now placed the family in

California. Thomas had been assigned to the 165th U.S. Army Aero Squadron, but sometime

in late January, soon after arrival, he became ill. He died on February 10th with the cause of

death being listed as: non-infectious cerebrospinal fever with acute otitis media added as a

contributory factor. His body was returned to Greenwood Memorial Park in San Diego,

California, where he lies in death today next to his father.

Thomas James Death Certificate

MARCH

March 21st saw the next casualty as John Ralph DesChamps from Michigan. He was a twenty-four-year-old salesman, listed in the 1910 U.S. Census as a newsboy. His draft card said he was selling to farmers in the Zeeland County area of Michigan. He was single, of medium build, with brown eyes and black hair. On March 7th, the airplane he was in crashed and by some miracle, John was not killed instantly. He was taken to the hospital where he lay for fourteen days. Pneumonia set in and eventually claimed the young life on March 21, 1918. His body was returned to his family where he was buried in Detroit, Michigan.

John Ralph Deschamps Death Certificate

Orrin G. Franks came to the war effort from Clyde, Ohio. He was born in Green Creek, Ohio on January 13, 1891. Before his induction into the military, he had worked at

Universal Paper Products, serving as a foreman in the box factory. He was a little older than some of the other pilots when he came to Call Field. Tall, of medium build, with brown eyes and dark hair that was beginning to show signs of balding, he died on the 27th of March when the aeroplane he was piloting exploded and fell burning to the ground killing Orrin instantly. He was among fifteen Clyde, Ohio men to die in World War I, and the town honored him by naming an American Legion after him.

Orrin Franks Obituary

AN IMPRESSIVE FUNERAL

Body of Clyde Aviator Killed in Texas Buried With Impressive Services.

The body of Orrin G. Franks, who was killed at Call aviation field at Wichita Falls, Texas, on Wednesday of last week, arrived in Clyde Saturday morning accompanied by Fred C. Goddard, a Michigan boy who was Orrin's chum and bosom friend, and to whom the field commander assigned the duty of bringing the body home and attending the obsequies. Dee Franks, brother of Orrin, went to Bellefontaine to meet the body, and to avoid a long delay in that city he succeeded in having it sent from there to Clyde via Toledo. The remains were taken to the home of the family, corner of George and Amanda Sts.,

and remained there until Sunday at two o'clock when the funeral services were held at the Methodist church, which could not hold nearly all those who wished to pay their last respects, many being unable to secure admission.

Monticello Lodge No. 244, F. & A. M. of which Orrin was a mem-

young men of Clyde have already been sacrificed in the war against the Huns. May the patriotism that cost them their lives bring home to our people the full significance of our duty to the country.

The following obituary, prepared by Supt. A. J. Love, was read at the church by Rev. Ridredge:

Orrin G. Franks was born Jan. 13, 1891. He spent his entire life in Clyde, with the exception of three years, which time the family lived in Bellevue.

Orrin attended the Bellevue High School through his Junior Year, but the following year, the family having moved back to Clyde, he entered the Clyde High School, in which he completed his Senior Year and graduated at the age of seventeen in the Class of '08.

He served as page in the House of Representatives at Columbus during the session of the General Assembly in 1911. Following this he was identified for some time with a commission house in that city. Later he worked for the Estill Grocery Co. in Clyde and resigned this place for the position of foreman in the stock room of the Universal Paper Products Co. He left this position to enlist in the army.

He enlisted on July 27, 1917, in the aviation corps. He reported at Columbus for duty and was assigned to the

¹PLACE OF DEATH

County _Wichita_

ell Field
City _Wichita Falls, Texas_ (No. ....St.; .... Ward)

TEXAS STATE BOARD OF HEALTH
Bureau of Vital Statistics

STANDARD CERTIFICATE OF DEATH

Registered No. **14508**

2423-316-50M

[If death occurred in a hospital or institution, give its NAME instead of street and number.]

²FULL NAME _Orin G. Franks, no. 1089830._

PERSONAL AND STATISTICAL PARTICULARS

3 SEX _M._	4 Color or Race _W._	5 Single, Married, Widowed, or Divorced (Write the word) _Single_

6 DATE OF BIRTH _January_ _14th_ _1891_
(Month) (Day) (Year)

7 AGE _27_ yrs. _2_ mos. _13_ ds.
If less than 2 years state if breast fed | If less than 1 day
Yes ____ No ____ | ____ hrs. ____ mins.

8 OCCUPATION
(a) Trade, profession, or particular kind of work _Soldier_
(b) General nature of industry, business, or establishment in which employed (or employer) ____

9 BIRTHPLACE (State or country) _Clyde, Ohio, U.S.A._

PARENTS	10 NAME OF FATHER	_Not Known_
	11 BIRTHPLACE OF FATHER (State or country)	_Not Known_
	12 MAIDEN NAME OF MOTHER	_Not Known_
	13 BIRTHPLACE OF MOTHER (State or country)	_Not Known_

14 THE ABOVE IS TRUE TO THE BEST OF MY KNOWLEDGE
(Informant) _Jas B Barksdale_
(Address) _2nd Lt Sig Rsv_

15

Filed _April 23, 1918_ _M.H. Moore_
Registrar

MEDICAL PARTICULARS

16 DATE OF DEATH _March_ _27_ _1918_
(Month) (Day) (Year)

17 I HEREBY CERTIFY, That I attended deceased from ...., 191...., to ...., 191....
that I last saw h.... alive on ...., 191....,
and that death occurred, on the date stated above, at _9 35_ a.m.
The CAUSE OF DEATH* was as follows:
Conflagration burning of airplane following explosion.
instaneous.

(Duration .... yrs .... mos. .... ds.)

Contributory (Secondary)

(Duration .... yrs .... mos. .... ds.)

(Signed) _Curtis Atkinson_ M. D.
Major M.R.C.
..........., 191.... (Address) _Call Field, Wichita Falls Texas_

*Use International List of Cause of Death—State the Disease Causing Death, or, in deaths from Violent Causes, State (1) Means of Injury; and (2) whether Accidental, Suicidal, or Homicidal.

18 LENGTH OF RESIDENCE (For Hospitals, Institutions, Transients, or Recent Residents)
At place of death .... yrs .... mos .... ds.
In the State .... yrs .... mos .... ds.
Where was disease contracted, if not at place of death? ....
Former or usual residence ....

19 PLACE OF BURIAL OR REMOVAL	DATE OF BURIAL
Clyde Ohio	..........., 191....
20 UNDERTAKER _Owens???_	ADDRESS _W falls_

Orrin Franks Death Certificate

APRIL

April 1st witnessed the death of another young pilot, Byron Jackson, Jr. of California. Byron was the only child in his family, and before the war, had been a salesman for the Bean Spray Pump Company.

He was a graduate of Lowell High School and the University of California. Having enlisted in San Francisco the previous November, Byron was in the Aviation Ground School at Berkeley until December 6. He was then transferred to the Military Aviation School at Call Field.

Receiving his commission the week before April 1st, he was immediately appointed as an instructor in flying. After spending a leave with his parents in San Francisco, he was immediately put in the field and had been taking cadets up all morning on the 1st, continuing that work into the afternoon. He and one cadet had been working on stunt flying.

According to the New York Times, Second Lieutenant Byron Jackson, Jr. was instantly killed at Call Field about 4:30 p.m. when the machine in which he was flying crashed to the earth from a distance of 1,500 feet out of control. A cadet who was with Lt. Jackson was slightly injured.

The Wichita Falls Times covered the story with more details. Jackson and the cadet, Ted E. Hall, were about 3 miles southwest of the field when the crash occurred. Hall received a broken arm and numerous bruises and cuts.

The article stated, "The cause of the accident is unknown, but the ship was in a spinning nose dive when the fall occurred. Jackson, who was in the front seat, was killed instantly." Hall was stunned by the fall and had no recollection of the events.

Byron Jackson Jr. Death Certificate

The last segment of the article shows the admiration and respect that was accorded the young cadet. "When the train left the station at 2 o'clock, bearing the body of the dead aviator and his friend, Lieutenant Francis McGiffin, who took the body back to San Francisco, Lieutenant Booth flew close over the train and dropped flowers from his plane. One platoon of cadets, 32 in number formed a military escort from Call Field to the station."

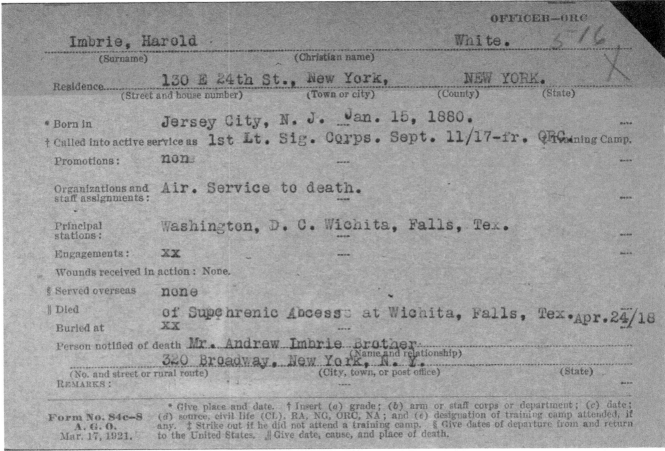

OFFICER—ORC

Imbrie, Harold   White. 5-16

(Surname)   (Christian name)

Residence   130 E 24th St., New York,   NEW YORK.

(Street and house number)   (Town or city)   (County)   (State)

* Born in   Jersey City, N. J. Jan. 15, 1880.

† Called into active service as 1st Lt. Sig. Corps. Sept. 11/17-fr. ORC Training Camp.

Promotions: none

Organizations and staff assignments: Air. Service to death.

Principal stations: Washington, D. C. Wichita, Falls, Tex.

Engagements: XX

Wounds received in action: None.

§ Served overseas   none

‖ Died   of Suprehrenic Abcess at Wichita, Falls, Tex. Apr. 24/18

Buried at   XX

Person notified of death Mr. Andrew Imbrie Brother.

(Name and relationship)

320 Broadway, New York, N. Y.

(No. and street or rural route)   (City, town, or post office)   (State)

REMARKS:

Form No. 84c-8   * Give place and date. † Insert (a) grade; (b) arm or staff corps or department; (c) date;
A. G. O.   (d) source, civil life (CL), RA, NG, ORC, NA; and (e) designation of training camp attended, if
Mar. 17, 1921.   any. ‡ Strike out if he did not attend a training camp. § Give dates of departure from and return
to the United States. ‖ Give date, cause, and place of death.

Harold Imbrie Service Record

Three casualties occurred on April 24th, but one had actually begun on March 6th.

Lieutenant Harold Imbrie was born January 15, 1890 in Jersey City, New Jersey. He lived a life of privilege as his father, after graduating from Princeton, had started out as a cotton exchange broker. The elder Imbrie married a wealthy New Jersey socialite whose father was an owner of a large fly-fishing equipment business. When his father died, Harold was brought into the business, and Abbey & Imbrie became a well-recognized name in sports equipment for fishermen.

Harold followed in his father's footsteps at Princeton University, but when the United States entered the war, he left his position as a broker at William Morris, Imbrie and Company and joined the war effort.

Like many others, he was beyond military age (38 years old), but he desired to enlist in service to his country and did so. He had been commissioned in September as a First Lieutenant in the non-flying branch of the Aviation Corps, the Signal Corps. He was assigned to Call Field . He first was Assistant to the Adjutant and afterward named Adjutant.

Before his service career, Harold was recognized for his talent with drawing. He had been editor of the school paper, *The Tiger*, and in later years continued as a free-lance illustrator for different publications, one of which was Life Magazine.

Harold Imbrie became ill on March 6th and was eventually transferred to the Wichita Falls General Hospital where he was cared for until April 24th when he succumbed to pneumonia. His mother had managed to get to him before his death and was there with him when he took his last breath.

His body was returned to New Jersey where his funeral was held in the Brick Presbyterian Church of New York on April 30th and was afterward interred in the Greenwood, New York.

The same day that Harold Imbrie died, an airplane crash at Call Field took the lives of two young pilots. The instructor for the flight was Steven Reed Warner, and the cadet was Edwin D. Cryer.

Warner was from New Haven, Connecticut. He had graduated from the Stevens Institute of Technology in Hoboken, New Jersey, where he was a member of the Phi Sigma Kappa Fraternity. Born in 1894, he was of medium height and build with brown eyes and dark hair. Arriving on his military journey from Maplewood, New Jersey, he became an air flight instructor at Call Field.

The cadet also involved in the crash was, as mentioned, Edwin D. Cryer of Allegheny County, Pennsylvania. Before his enlistment, he was Agency Secretary for Philadelphia Life Insurance Company. At age 26, he attended the School of Military Aeronautics/Aviation Ground School at Ohio State University in Columbus, Ohio. He enlisted in the Aviation Signal Corps in December, coming to Call Field on December 17th.

According to an Associated Press Report, the crash occurred two miles east of Call Field, when their plane flying 50 feet above ground, suddenly burst into flames and fell. Both bodies were badly burned, and the cause of death was listed a conflagration from a burning airplane.

PLANE CATCHES FIRE; TWO AVIATORS PERISH

WICHITA FALLS, Tex., April 24.— Second Lieutenant Stephen R. Warner, flying instructor of Maplewood, N. J., and Cadet Ed D. Cryer, of Allegheny county, Pa., were killed two miles of Call Field, near here, this morning, when their plane fell. Both bodies were badly burned.

Warner was buried in Woodlawn Cemetery and Conservancy in Bronx, New York. Cryer was interred in Fernwood, Pennsylvania. With their deaths, as well as Harold Imbrie's, the day of April 24, 1918, finally ended at Call Field.

				8
Cryer, (Surname)	Edwin D (Christian name)	1,089,510 (Army serial number)	*White *Colored	

Residence: 1421 Arch St (Street and house number) Philadelphia (Town or city) (County) PENNSYLVANIA (State)

*Enlisted *R. A. *N. G. *E. R. C. *Inducted at Essington Pa on Sept 8, 19 17

Place of birth: Philadelphia Pa   Age or date of birth: 26 2/12 yrs

Organizations served in, with dates of assignments and transfers:
School of Military Aeronautics Ohio State University to Dec 4/17; Call Field Wichita Falls Tex to death

Grades, with date of appointment:
Pvt 1c1

Engagements:

Wounds or other injuries received in action: *None.   ACTIVE DUTY FROM 9-29-17

Served overseas from †   to †   , from †   to †

Died of conflagration from burning airplane   Apr 24/18, 19
(Cause and date of death)

Person notified of death: Chas W Cryer (Name)   Brother (Degree of relationship)

205 N 6 St (No. and street or rural route)   Philadelphia (City, town, or post office)   Pa (State or country)

Remarks: P N P

Form No. 724-8, A. G. O.   *Strike out words not applicable.   †Dates of departure from and arrival in the U.S.
Nov. 22, 1919.   3—7369

MAY

STANDARD CERTIFICATE OF DEATH

DEPARTMENT OF COMMERCE
BUREAU OF THE CENSUS

1 PLACE OF DEATH County *Wichita* , State *Texas* Registered No. _____

Township _____ or Village _____ or
City *Wichita Falls* No. *Post Hospital Call Field* St. _____ Ward _____
(If death occurred in a hospital or institution, give its NAME instead of street and number)

23075

2 FULL NAME *Clarence L. Stevens no 1184190*

(a) Residence. No. *Call Field* St. _____ Ward _____
(Usual place of abode)
Length of residence in city or town where death occurred ___ yrs. ___ mos. ___ ds. How long in U. S., if of foreign birth? ___ yrs. ___ mos. ___ ds.

PERSONAL AND STATISTICAL PARTICULARS	MEDICAL CERTIFICATE OF DEATH
3 SEX *male* 4 COLOR OR RACE *white* 5 SINGLE, MARRIED, WIDOWED, OR DIVORCED (write the word) *married*	16 DATE OF DEATH (month, day, and year) *May 1* 19*18*

17 I HEREBY CERTIFY, That I attended deceased from *April 20*, 19*18* to *May 1*, 19*18*

5a If married, widowed, or divorced
HUSBAND of (or WIFE of) *Elfie Julia Stevens*

that I last saw him alive on *May 1* 19*18*
and that death occurred, on the date stated above, at *5-8* ___ m.

6 DATE OF BIRTH (month, day, and year) *Apr. 30, 1898*

The CAUSE OF DEATH* was as follows:
Lobar Pneumonia

7 AGE Years *20* Months *0* Days *1* If LESS than 1 day, ___ hrs. or ___ min.

(10)

8 OCCUPATION OF DECEASED
(a) Trade, profession, or particular kind of work *Soldier*
(b) General nature of industry, business, or establishment in which employed (or employer) *U.S. Sig. C., S.C.*
(c) Name of employer _____

(duration) ___ yrs. ___ mos. *9* ds.
CONTRIBUTORY (SECONDARY) *Influenza*
(duration) ___ yrs. ___ mos. *2* ds.

18 Where was disease contracted if not at place of death? _____
Did an operation precede death? *no* Date of _____
Was there an autopsy? *no*
What test confirmed diagnosis? _____

9 BIRTHPLACE (city or town) *New York City*
(State or country)

(Signed) *Curtis Atkinson* , M. D.

10 NAME OF FATHER ✓

, 19 (Address) *Call Field, Wichita Falls, Texas.*

11 BIRTHPLACE OF FATHER (city or town) ✓
(State or country)

* State the DISEASE CAUSING DEATH, or in deaths from VIOLENT CAUSES, state (1) MEANS AND NATURE OF INJURY, and (2) whether ACCIDENTAL, SUICIDAL, or HOMICIDAL. (See reverse side for additional space.)

12 MAIDEN NAME OF MOTHER ✓

13 BIRTHPLACE OF MOTHER (city or town) ✓
(State or country)

14 Informant *John B.E. Wheeler*
(Address) *2nd Lt. Sig. R.C. A.S., Call Field Wichita Falls Texas*

19 PLACE OF BURIAL, CREMATION, OR REMOVAL | DATE OF BURIAL , 19

15 Filed _____ , 19 _____ REGISTRAR

20 UNDERTAKER | ADDRESS

Clarence Stevens Death Certificate

At 20, he started his military service on January 25, 1917, stationed at Fort Slocum, New York. He served there until he was reassigned to the 56 Rct. Sq. Aviation Camp in Waco, Texas on February 25, 1918.

It is uncertain when he arrived at Call Field, but he reported sick on April 20th. Under the care of Dr. Curtis Atkinson at the post hospital, he died on May 1st from lobar pneumonia with a contributory cause listed as influenza.

The first day of May saw the next casualty for Call Field. Clarence L. Stevens was born April 20, 1898 in New York City to Edwin and Ella Stevens.

May 18th saw the next casualty, a fiery plane crash which took the life of Jerome Trace Van Auken. Van Auken was born on January 15, 1896 in Saginaw, Michigan to Willis and Florence Van Auken. He was the fourth child and had five other siblings.

He attended Saginaw High School and appears in the 1915 yearbook with the inscription beneath his picture, "Happy am I; from care I am free! Why aren't they all content like me?" After graduation, he worked as a bookkeeper according to the 1916 Salt Lake City, Utah, city directory, going west to seek adventure. At the time of his entry into military service, he was working as a lumberman.

Van Auken

Crash

Van Auken arrived at Call Field in January of 1918 and quickly learned about airships. However, on May 18th that knowledge and skill were tested beyond their limits, and another pilot had listed on his death certificate, "conflagration, burning airplane."

Jerome Trace Van Auken is buried in Oakwood Cemetery in his beloved hometown of Saginaw, Michigan, another one of America's finest young men lost in the war effort.

Jerome T. Van Auken Death Certificate

JUNE

Remarkably, in June of 1918 no deaths were recorded at Call Field. Maybe, it seemed the worst was over, or maybe it was just the calm before the storm. One can imagine the anxiety that rested with each pilot as they took off from the dirt runway, wondering if this would be their last flight or not.

JULY

Death only took some time off as it appeared again on July 4th, our nation's observance of Independence Day. It came to a young soldier named William H. Lees.

William had been born June 20, 1892 in Salt Lake City, Utah. The 1900 U.S. Census lists him living with his mother, Agnes, and three other siblings. His draft registration card described him as being of medium build, with blues eyes and dark brown hair. At the time his occupation was salesman for the Acme White Lead and Color Company.

He had enlisted at for Fort Douglas, Utah on December 15, 1917, as the United States' involvement in World War I heightened.

At Call Field, he was in the Aviation Section as a mechanic. On June 22, Lees fell ill and died on July 4, 1918, a victim of acute nephritis. His remains were laid to rest in the city of his beginning, Salt Lake City, Utah.

STANDARD CERTIFICATE OF DEATH

DEPARTMENT OF COMMERCE
BUREAU OF THE CENSUS

1 PLACE OF DEATH

County _Wichita_ State _Texas_ Registered No. _____

Township _Wichita Falls_ or Village _Post._ _Call Field_

City _Wichita Falls_ No. ____, _____ St., ____ Ward

(If death occurred in a hospital or institution, give its NAME instead of street and number)

2 FULL NAME _William H Lees_

(a) Residence. No. _Call Field Wichita Falls._ 7e4. Ward. __3_251__

(Usual place of abode)

(If nonresident give city or town and State)

Length of residence in city or town where death occurred _0_ yrs. _4_ mos. _4_ ds. How long in U. S., if of foreign birth? _~_ yrs. _—_ mos. _—_ ds.

PERSONAL AND STATISTICAL PARTICULARS	MEDICAL CERTIFICATE OF DEATH

3 SEX _male_

4 COLOR OR RACE _white_

5 SINGLE, MARRIED, WIDOWED, OR DIVORCED (write the word) _Single_

16 DATE OF DEATH (month, day, and year) 19

17 I HEREBY CERTIFY, That I attended deceased from _June 22_, 19_18_, to _July 4_, 19_18_,

that I last saw h~im~ alive on _July 3_, 19_18_,

and that death occurred, on the date stated above, at _12 ½ a._m.

5a If married, widowed, or divorced
HUSBAND of
(or) WIFE of _____

The CAUSE OF DEATH* was as follows:

Nephritis acute

6 DATE OF BIRTH (month, day, and year) _June 20 1892._

7 AGE Years _26_ Months _~_ Days _14_ If LESS than 1 day, ... hrs. or 12 min.

_____ (duration) .... yrs. ...... mos. ...... ds.

8 OCCUPATION OF DECEASED

(a) Trade, profession, or particular kind of work _Mechanic_

(b) General nature of industry, business, or establishment in which employed (or employer) _Aviation Section US._

(c) Name of employer

CONTRIBUTORY
(SECONDARY)

_____ (duration) ...... yrs. ...... mos. ...... ds.

18 Where was disease contracted if not at place of death? _____

9 BIRTHPLACE (city or town) _Salt Lake City Utah_
(State or country)

Did an operation precede death? _No_ Date of _____

Was there an autopsy? _Yes_

10 NAME OF FATHER _not available_

What test confirmed diagnosis? _____

11 BIRTHPLACE OF FATHER (city or town) _not known_
(State or country)

(Signed) _Curtis Atkinson_ M. D.

12 MAIDEN NAME OF MOTHER _Not known_

,19 (Address) _Call Field Wichita Falls Texas_

13 BIRTHPLACE OF MOTHER (city or town) _Not known_
(State or country)

* State the DISEASE CAUSING DEATH, or in deaths from VIOLENT CAUSES, state (1) MEANS AND NATURE OF INJURY, and (2) whether ACCIDENTAL, SUICIDAL, or HOMICIDAL. (See reverse side for additional space.)

14 Informant _Jos. L Black_
(Address) _Call Field Texas_

19 PLACE OF BURIAL, CREMATION, OR REMOVAL ✓

DATE OF BURIAL ✓ 19

15 Filed _Aug 9_; 19_8_ _CW Beckman_
REGISTRAR

20 UNDERTAKER _O W Kinns Wichita Falls_

ADDRESS

William H. Lees Death Certificate

45

Harry Shelmire Ross, '18.

On July 12th, another airplane crash took the life of a pilot at Call Field. Harry Shelmire Ross was that unfortunate pilot. Ross had been born December 13, 1894 in Philadelphia, Pennsylvania to Edwin and Maude Shelmire Ross. According to the 1910 census, the family was living with Edwin Ross's father, William. William is listed as a recorder and Edwin as an assistant recorder.

The Eau Claire, Wisconsin newspaper carried a news brief with the headlines, "AMERICAN AIRMAN KILLED IN FALL AT CALL FIELD. Dateline July 11, 1918…Second Lieutenant Harry J. (error should have been S.) Ross, an instructor, was killed today when his plane fell at Call Field. His home was in Philadelphia, PA. Lieutenant Sigurd A. Emerson, the other occupant of the machine was not seriously injured. The plane fell only about 100 feet."

Twenty-three-year-old Harry Ross' remains were returned to his hometown of Philadelphia where they were interred at Northwood Cemetery, leaving another family left to mourn the loss of a loved one to the war effort.

Harry S. Ross Death Certificate

Ross Crash

AUGUST

Death is a tragedy. All the deaths at Call Field snuffed out the flames of youth and promise. Still, the airplane crash on August 30, 1918, which took the lives of two aviators was of huge significance. The instructor was Francis Roy McGiffin, and the young cadet was Ellis Babcock.

Here are their stories.

If you read between the lines of the history of Call Field, Francis Roy McGiffin emerges as one of the most respected and likely feared men on the post. He was born in 1890 in Canada.

According to his Declaration of Intention signed in 1913, he arrived in the United States at Seattle on the Princess Victoria and was living in Fresno, California working as a fruit inspector. On the document, he renounced his citizenship as an English subject and pledged his loyalty to the United States.

The untold details of the document, however, were the most important. Francis Roy "Minnie" McGiffin was a professional hockey player and a really good one at that.

He played amateur hockey in Toronto beginning at age 15. He had played the 1911-12 season for Cleveland of the United States Amateur Hockey Association, before turning professional with the Toronto Blueshirts. He was a member of the 1914 Stanley Cup Championship Blueshirts.

In the 1914 Stanley Cup challenge of Victoria against the Blueshirts, McGiffin scored the game winning goal in game two. Minnie was a good player, but until research was done, it was not known his real role on the team. Minnie was 'the enforcer." At five foot eight and 155 pounds with brown hair and hazel eyes, he was a sight on the ice. While playing in the National Hockey Association from 1913 to 1915, he led the league in penalties. In the 60-minutes game time, McGiffin spent over 9 to 14 minutes in the penalty box.

In a February 17, 1915 game against the Ottawa Senators, McGiffin and Art Ross became involved in a fight that ended with both players being arrested and sent to jail. Each were fined $1; they tossed a coin; Minnie lost and paid both fines. Cooper Smeaton, the referee of the game, wanted McGiffin barred from the league.

Francis Roy McGiffin was a fighter and feared by many. After the 1914-15 season, Minnie decided to retire and go into business in Dinuba, California. In June of 1917, he married Lillian Schroeder of San Francisco and seemed to settle down until the United States entered World War I, and Minnie McGiffin was given the chance for one last fight.

He became an instructor at Call Field, and perhaps the reader might remember, he accompanied the body of Byron Jackson, Jr. back to California. Yes, Francis Roy McGiffin was a notable presence at Call Field.

Ellis Babcock was the cadet McGiffin was training that day. He was born January 23, 1897 in New York. His father was Colonel W.C. Babcock, who at the time of the accident was with American forces in France. Ellis, or Ellie, as the family called him, had graduated from West Point and was listed as a teacher in civilian life.

When the U.S. entered the war, Ellie joined the war effort and was sent to Call Field to learn aviation. Since his father was in Europe fighting in the war, his mother, Mary, accompanied him to Texas, leaving behind her residence in the Cairo Apartments in Washington DC.

Babcock was in his first flight lesson with his instructor, the infamous Francis Roy "Minnie" McGiffin. They were endeavoring, according to newspaper accounts, to master a complicated dive from 2,000 feet. The plane failed, and they fell to their deaths. The Death Certificate listed as cause of death for both, "compound fracture of skull, accidental airplane crash." McGiffin's body was returned to Mountain View Cemetery in Fresno, California, and Ellis Babcock's remains were sent to Washington DC, where he was interred in Arlington National Cemetery.

Francis "Minnie" McGriffin Death Certificate

TEXAS STATE BOARD OF HEALTH
BUREAU OF VITAL STATISTICS
STANDARD CERTIFICATE OF DEATH

1 PLACE OF DEATH

County _Wichita_

Reg. Dis. No. _____

Registered No. **32973**

B.O.V.S. FORM D

City _Wichita Falls, Texas_ (No. _Call Field_ St.; _____ Ward)

2 FULL NAME _Ellis B Babcock, no. 24 84 015_ (a) RESIDENCE. No. _Cairo apts_ St. _Washington D.C._
(If nonresident give city or town and State)

Length of residence in city or town where death occurred ___ yrs ___ mos ___ ds. How long in U. S., if of foreign birth? ___ yrs ___ mos ___ ds

PERSONAL AND STATISTICAL PARTICULARS	MEDICAL PARTICULARS

PERSONAL AND STATISTICAL PARTICULARS

3 SEX _Male_

4 COLOR OR RACE _White_

5 SINGLE, MARRIED, WIDOWED OR DIVORCED (write the word) _Single_

6 DATE OF BIRTH _Jan_ (Month) _23_ (Day) _1897_ (Year)

7 AGE _21_ yrs. _8_ mos. _6_ ds.
If less than 2 years state if breast fed | If less than 1 day
Yes ___ No ___ | ___ hrs. ___ mins.

8 OCCUPATION
(a) Trade, profession or particular kind of work _Teacher in civil life_
(b) General nature of industry, business or establishment in which employed (or employer)

9 BIRTHPLACE (State or country) _West Point, N.Y_

10 NAME OF FATHER _W. C. Babcock_

11 BIRTHPLACE OF FATHER (State or country)

12 MAIDEN NAME OF MOTHER

13 BIRTHPLACE OF MOTHER (State or country)

PARENTS

14 THE ABOVE IS TRUE
(Informant) _1st Lieut J K Harner A S Sig RC_
(Address) _Cal Field Wichita Falls Tex_

15 Filed _Sep 3, 1918_ _M A Berkman_ Registrar

MEDICAL PARTICULARS

16 DATE OF DEATH _Aug_ (Month) _30_ (Day) _1918_ (Year)

17 I HEREBY CERTIFY, That I attended deceased from _____, 19___, to _____, 19___
that I last saw him alive on _____, 19___
and that death occurred, on the date stated above, at _7:5-0_ A.m.
The CAUSE OF DEATH was as follows:
Compound fracture of skull, accidental airplane crash
_____ (duration) ___ yrs. ___ mos. ___ ds.

Contributory (Secondary)
_____ (duration) ___ yrs. ___ mos. ___ ds.

18 Where was disease contracted if not at place of death? _____
Did an operation precede death? ___ Date of ___
Was there an autopsy? ___
What test confirmed diagnosis? ___
(Signed) _Curtis Atkinson 1st Lt M.R.C._ M. D.
Aug 31, 19_18_ (Address) _Call Field Wichita Falls Texas_

*State the Disease Causing Death, or in deaths from Violent Causes, state (1) Means and Nature of Injury, and (2) whether Accidental, Suicidal, or Homicidal. (See reverse side for State Statutes.)

19 PLACE OF BURIAL OR REMOVAL _Washington D C_

DATE OF BURIAL _Sept_ 191_8_

20 UNDERTAKER _W B Hines_ ADDRESS _W Falls_

E. L. STECK, AUSTIN

2127-218-50M

Ellis Babcock Death Certificate

Ellis Babcock &
Francis McGriffin Crash

SEPTEMBER

The month of September came and went with no deaths. Fourteen lives were enough to have been lost, but no one could foresee the ravages that would come in the fall/winter of 1918.

Until now, airplane crashes and a medical condition had been the contributing factors for all the losses. Now, a new health factor raised its head and cried out for victims. That enemy would be the Spanish Flu epidemic that was taking lives, not only in the United States but throughout the world.

"The Spanish Flu pandemic claimed between 20 to 25 million lives." Oddly enough, it probably didn't start in Spain but possibility in China, the British military camps, or even Haskell, Kansas. There were actually two stages, or waves, that surfaced.

The first was in the spring of 1918; the second occurred in the fall and winter. That was the one that hit Call Field and the Wichita Falls area. Some sources say it began with a newly arrived squadron from Cruthers Field in Fort Worth, Texas. Whatever the origin, the disease was deadly.

The first stage of the illness was characterized in actually two stages. The first saw the patient complaining of aching joints, dry cough, runny nose, and diarrhea. This initial stage opened the door for the second stage, which would be the onset of pneumonia.

The second full stage led to the name of the disease as the purple death because it turned the patient blue due to a lack of oxygen and the coughing up of a bloody sputum. Temperatures would rise to 100-104 degrees.

The oddity of the flu was that it affected healthy adults between the ages of 18 and 40, turning the body's immune system against itself.

Generally, flu affects the young and elderly first, but this one went after people in the prime of life, just like the servicemen at Call Field.

The brand new Wichita Falls General Hospital soon saw its 30 beds filled to capacity, so Wichita County, under Judge Harris, offered the upper rooms of the courthouse to house influenza victims, amidst the protest of county employees who worked there.

"On October 4th, there were only five cases of the Spanish Flu that had been reported. Three days later on the 7th, 100 cases had been diagnosed, and by October 11th, 1,000 cases ravaged the city.

The movie theaters, stock exchange, and schools, were promptly closed, and assemblies of any kind were strongly discouraged. The shortage of physicians made the city officials pleas for community members to help out, which many women in the community did."[4]

The Spanish Flu was a pandemic, sometimes referred to as "the Mother of all Pandemics." Scientists believe that it was the first flu virus that originated with birds and then skipped to the human species. It was something that was to be feared, and by October 12th, it had arrived in full force at Call Field.

OCTOBER

STANDARD CERTIFICATE OF DEATH

DEPARTMENT OF COMMERCE
BUREAU OF THE CENSUS

1 PLACE OF DEATH
County _Wichita_ State _Texas_ Registered No. ____
Township _Call Field_ or Village ____ 46881 or
City _Wichita Falls_ No. _Post Hospital Call Field Texas_ B Ward
(If death occurred in a hospital or institution, give its NAME instead of street and number)

2 FULL NAME _Philip T. Whittle_
(a) Residence. No. _Call Field Texas_ St. B Ward. ____
(Usual place of abode) (If nonresident give city or town and State)
Length of residence in city or town where death occurred yrs. mos. 23 ds. How long in U. S., if of foreign birth? yrs. mos. ds.

PERSONAL AND STATISTICAL PARTICULARS | MEDICAL CERTIFICATE OF DEATH

3 SEX _Male_ | 4 COLOR OR RACE _White_ | 5 SINGLE, MARRIED, WIDOWED, OR DIVORCED (write the word) _Single_

16 DATE OF DEATH (month, day, and year) _Oct 12_ 19_18_

5a If married, widowed, or divorced
HUSBAND of
(or) WIFE of ____

17 I HEREBY CERTIFY, That I attended deceased from _Oct 5_, 19_18_, to _Oct 12_, 19_18_,
that I last saw him alive on _Oct 12_, 19_18_
and that death occurred, on the date stated above, at _3 A._m.

6 DATE OF BIRTH (month, day, and year) _Dec. 22 - 1893_

7 AGE Years 24 | Months 9 | Days 10 | If LESS than 1 day, ---- hrs. or ---- min.

The CAUSE OF DEATH* was as follows:
Pneumonia, lobular

8 OCCUPATION OF DECEASED
(a) Trade, profession, or particular kind of work _Student_
(b) General nature of industry, business, or establishment in which employed (or employer) _Not Known_
(c) Name of employer

(duration) ---- yrs. ---- mos. 9 ds.
CONTRIBUTORY _Influenza, epidemic_
(SECONDARY)
(duration) ---- yrs. ---- mos. 5 ds.

9 BIRTHPLACE (city or town) _Worcester Mass._
(State or country)

18 Where was disease contracted if not at place of death? ____
Did an operation precede death? _no_ Date of ____
Was there an autopsy? _no_
What test confirmed diagnosis? ____
(Signed) _Curtis Atkinson_, M. D.
, 19 (Address) _Call Field Wichita Falls Texas._

PARENTS
10 NAME OF FATHER _Not Known_
11 BIRTHPLACE OF FATHER (city or town) _Not Known_
(State or country)
12 MAIDEN NAME OF MOTHER _Not Known_
13 BIRTHPLACE OF MOTHER (city or town) _Not Known_
(State or country)

* State the DISEASE CAUSING DEATH, or in deaths from VIOLENT CAUSES, state (1) MEANS AND NATURE OF INJURY, and (2) whether ACCIDENTAL, SUICIDAL, or HOMICIDAL. (See reverse side for additional space.)

14 Informant _George Southworth_
(Address) _2nd Lt ASC_

19 PLACE OF BURIAL, CREMATION, OR REMOVAL | DATE OF BURIAL 19

15 Filed _3 - 7_, 19_19_ _M. C. Beckman_
REGISTRAR

20 UNDERTAKER | ADDRESS

Phillip T. Whittle Death Certificate

Phillip T. Whittle would be the first of six who would die from the ravages of the illness

in that month alone. Phillip had been born December 22, 1893 in Worchester, Massachusetts

to James Henry and Louisa Starrett Whittle. His father James was listed as a manufacturer of

tire cylinders, and the family had a servant living with them as listed in the 1910 census.

Louisa had died by this time, and James had remarried a younger woman, Bertha.

Phillip was more than likely a child of privilege to some extent. He had only been in the city for a total of 16 days when he fell ill to the flu epidemic. He entered the post hospital on October 5th and died there a week later on October 12th. The cause of death was listed as pneumonia, lobular, and the contributory factor was the influenza epidemic.

The next day, George Williams became the second death for the month of October. George had been born March 3, 1891 in Trenton, New Jersey to Henry and Margaret Williams. By 1910, his father had died, and George lived with his mother and worked as a "pottery thrower." However, by the time he registered for military service, he had married Leona Catherine Kenney and was working as a tire maker for Empire Tire and Rubber Company in Trenton.

According to his registration card, he was of medium height and weight with blue eyes and brown hair. It is not known how long George was at the post before he fell ill, but we do know he was under the doctor's care beginning October 6th, the week before his death. The death certificate lists his date of death as October 13th and attributed it to pneumonia, lobular, with the contributory factor being the influenza epidemic.

His body was returned to Trenton, New Jersey, where the local newspaper reported, **"BRING SOLDIER'S BODY TO TRENTON FOR BURIAL…"** "Word has been received here of the death of Private George Williams, Air Service, National Army. The body will arrive here today, and the funeral will be held from the home of his sister, 1019 Brunswick Avenue, at a time to be announced later. Donahoe is in charge. Williams was formerly employed in the plant of the Empire Rubber Company." After his funeral, the body was interred in Saint Mary's Cemetery in Trenton.

STANDARD CERTIFICATE OF DEATH

DEPARTMENT OF COMMERCE
BUREAU OF THE CENSUS

1 PLACE OF DEATH

County _Wichita_ State _Texas._ Registered No. _46880_

Township _Call Field_ or Village _____

City _Wichita Falls_ No. _Cost Hospital Call Field Tex_ St., _A_ Ward
(If death occurred in a hospital or institution, give its NAME instead of street and number)

2 FULL NAME _George Williams_ no. _1148830_

(a) Residence. No. _Call Field_ St., _A_ Ward. _Wichita Falls, Tex._
(Usual place of abode) (If nonresident give city or town and State)

Length of residence in city or town where death occurred ___ yrs. ___ mos. ___ ds. How long in U. S., if of foreign birth? ___ yrs. ___ mos. ___ ds.

PERSONAL AND STATISTICAL PARTICULARS	MEDICAL CERTIFICATE OF DEATH

3 SEX _Male_ **4 COLOR OR RACE** _White_ **5 SINGLE, MARRIED, WIDOWED, OR DIVORCED** (write the word) _Married_

16 DATE OF DEATH (month, day, and year) _Oct 13_ 19_18_

17 I HEREBY CERTIFY, That I attended deceased from _Oct 6_, 19_18_, to _Oct 13_, 19_18_,

that I last saw him alive on _Oct 13_, 19_18_,

and that death occurred, on the date stated above, at _10 30_ A.m.

5a If married, widowed, or divorced (Pending)

HUSBAND of (or) WIFE of _Leona Catherine Kenney Williams._

6 DATE OF BIRTH (month, day, and year) _March - 3 - 1891_

7 AGE Years _27_ Months _7_ Days _10_ If LESS than 1 day, ---- hrs. or ---- min.

The CAUSE OF DEATH* was as follows: _Pneumonia, labular_

8 OCCUPATION OF DECEASED

(a) Trade, profession, or particular kind of work _Vulcanizer._

(b) General nature of industry, business, or establishment in which employed (or employer) _Tire Manufacturing_

(c) Name of employer

(duration) ___ yrs. ___ mos. _3_ ds.

CONTRIBUTORY (SECONDARY) _Epidemic Influenza_

(duration) ___ yrs. ___ mos. _7_ ds.

9 BIRTHPLACE (city or town) _Trenton New Jersey._
(State or country)

18 Where was disease contracted if not at place of death? _a_

Did an operation precede death? _no_ Date of _✓_

PARENTS

10 NAME OF FATHER _Not Known._

Was there an autopsy? _no_

11 BIRTHPLACE OF FATHER (city or town) _Not Known._
(State or country) _Conn._

What test confirmed diagnosis? _✓_

(Signed) _Curtis Atkinson_, M. D.

12 MAIDEN NAME OF MOTHER _Not Known._

,19 (Address) _Call Field, Wichita Falls Texas._

13 BIRTHPLACE OF MOTHER (city or town) _Not Known_
(State or country) _Ireland._

* State the DISEASE CAUSING DEATH, or in deaths from VIOLENT CAUSES, state (1) MEANS AND NATURE OF INJURY, and (2) whether ACCIDENTAL, SUICIDAL, or HOMICIDAL. (See reverse side for additional space.)

14 Informant _George C Southworth._
(Address) _2nd 76/ a.88 C. Comdy, 5 Sqn._

19 PLACE OF BURIAL, CREMATION, OR REMOVAL _✓_ **DATE OF BURIAL** _✓_ 19

15 Filed _2-7_, 19_19_ _M. C. Beckman_
REGISTRAR

20 UNDERTAKER _✓_ **ADDRESS** _✓_

George Williams Death Certificate

STANDARD CERTIFICATE OF DEATH

DEPARTMENT OF COMMERCE
BUREAU OF THE CENSUS

1 PLACE OF DEATH
County _Wichita_ State _Texas._ Registered No. _____
Township _Call Field_ or Village _____ or
City _Wichita Falls._ No. _Post Hospital Call Field Byst., A._ Ward
(If death occurred in a hospital or institution, give its NAME instead of street and number)

2 FULL NAME _Eugene V. Rhodes No 1184637._

(a) Residence. No. _Call Field_ St., _A._ Ward. _____ _46870_
(Usual place of abode) (If nonresident give city or town and State)
Length of residence in city or town where death occurred yrs. mos. ds. How long in U. S., if of foreign birth? yrs. mos. ds.

PERSONAL AND STATISTICAL PARTICULARS	MEDICAL CERTIFICATE OF DEATH

3 SEX _Male_ **4 COLOR OR RACE** _White_ **5 SINGLE, MARRIED, WIDOWED, OR DIVORCED** (write the word) _Single_

16 DATE OF DEATH (month, day, and year) _Oct 14_ 19_18_

17 I HEREBY CERTIFY, That I attended deceased from _Oct 6_, 19_18_, to _Oct 14_, 19_18_,

5a If married, widowed, or divorced HUSBAND of (or) WIFE of _____

that I last saw him alive on _Oct 14_ 19_18_, and that death occurred, on the date stated above, at _9_ P. m.

6 DATE OF BIRTH (month, day, and year) _May-23-1895_

The CAUSE OF DEATH* was as follows:
Pneumonia, lobular

7 AGE Years _23_ Months _4_ Days _22_ If LESS than 1 day, ---- hrs. or ---- min.

(duration) — yrs. — mos. _3_ ds.
CONTRIBUTORY (SECONDARY) _Influenza_

8 OCCUPATION OF DECEASED
(a) Trade, profession, or particular kind of work _Machinist._
(b) General nature of industry, business, or establishment in which employed (or employer) _Standard Sanitary Mfg Co._
(c) Name of employer

(duration) — yrs. — mos. _5_ ds.
18 Where was disease contracted if not at place of death? _____
Did an operation precede death? _no_ Date of _____
Was there an autopsy? _no_
What test confirmed diagnosis? _____

9 BIRTHPLACE (city or town) _Beaver_
(State or country) _Penn'a._

(Signed) _Curtis Atkinson_ M. D.
, 19 (Address) _Call Field, Wichita Falls, Texas_

10 NAME OF FATHER _J. F. Rhodes_

*State the DISEASE CAUSING DEATH, or in deaths from VIOLENT CAUSES, state (1) MEANS AND NATURE OF INJURY, and (2) whether ACCIDENTAL, SUICIDAL, or HOMICIDAL. (See reverse side for additional space.)

11 BIRTHPLACE OF FATHER (city or town) _____
(State or country) _Penn'a_

12 MAIDEN NAME OF MOTHER _Mary Gregg_

13 BIRTHPLACE OF MOTHER (city or town) _____
(State or country) _Penn'a_

14 Informant _George Southworth_
(Address) _2nd Lt Asst Chf Quartr_

19 PLACE OF BURIAL, CREMATION, OR REMOVAL ✓ **DATE OF BURIAL** ✓ 19

15 Filed _2-7_, 19_19_ _M. A. Beckman_ REGISTRAR

20 UNDERTAKER ✓ **ADDRESS** ✓

Eugene Verne Rhodes Death Certificate

The next day, October 14th, death claimed another young soldier. Eugene Verne Rhodes was born May 23, 1895 in West Bridgewater, Pennsylvania to J.F. and Mary Gregg Rhodes.

His father was a machinist, and Eugene grew up to follow in his footsteps, working for the Standard Sanitary Manufacturing Company in New Brighton, a company that made bathroom fixtures. On his registration card in 1917, he is listed as being of medium height and slender build, with blue eyes and dark hair.

Rhodes entered the service on September 12, 1917, first at Kelly Field but was, at some point, reassigned to Squadron D at Call Field. He fell ill on October 6th, 1918 and eight days later died in the post hospital. Cause of death was listed as pneumonia, lobular, with influenza listed as the contributory factor.

Eugene V. Rhodes' body was sent to Beaver County, Pennsylvania, where he was interred in the Grandview Cemetery. Records show that in 1934, Eugene's mother, Mary, with assistance from the American Legion, filed an application for veteran's compensation based on Eugene's service. She did receive an allotment of $10 a month for 20 months, a total of $200.

On October 16th the next loss of life occurred. Robert Farren, Jr. was born March 18, 1895 in Woodbridge, New Jersey to his parents, Robert Farren, Sr. and Margaret Rudd Farren. According to his registration card for World War I, he was a "box maker" for L.R. Donahue in Avenel, New Jersey. He was medium height and build with light hair and brown eyes.

From the 7th of October until his death on the 16th, Robert lay ill in the post hospital at Call Field fighting for his life. On the morning of the 16th at 5:45 a.m. that fight was over.

Robert Farren, Jr. Death Certificate

Cause of death was all too familiar now, pneumonia, lobular with the contributory

factor influenza epidemic. As in other death certificates, Dr. Curtis Atkinson, a major, signed

the paper, and the body was returned to Woodbridge, New Jersey, where he was laid to rest in

the Episcopal Cemetery.

STANDARD CERTIFICATE OF DEATH

DEPARTMENT OF COMMERCE
BUREAU OF THE CENSUS

1 PLACE OF DEATH *Wichita*

County .... State *Texas* .... Registered No. ....

Township *Call Field* .... or Village .... or

City *Wichita F'alls* .... No. .... St., *6* Ward

(If death occurred in a hospital or institution, give its NAME instead of street and number)

2 FULL NAME *Heber H. Thomas; No. 8 92 15 3*

46883

(a) Residence. No. *Call Field* St., *6* Ward ....

(Usual place of abode) (If nonresident give city or town and State)

Length of residence in city or town where death occurred ...... yrs. ...... mos. ...... ds. How long in U. S., if of foreign birth? ...... yrs. ...... mos. ...... ds.

PERSONAL AND STATISTICAL PARTICULARS	MEDICAL CERTIFICATE OF DEATH

3 SEX *Male* | **4 COLOR OR RACE** *White* | **5 SINGLE, MARRIED, WIDOWED, OR DIVORCED** (write the word) *Married*

16 DATE OF DEATH (month, day, and year) *Oct 17* 19*18*

5a If married, widowed, or divorced HUSBAND of (or) ~~WIFE of~~ *Virlie Lambourne Thomas*

17 I HEREBY CERTIFY, That I attended deceased from *Oct 9*, 19*18*, to *Oct 17*, 19*18*, that I last saw him alive on *Oct 17*, 19*18*, and that death occurred, on the date stated above, at *2¹⁵ A.*m.

6 DATE OF BIRTH (month, day, and year) *May - 24 - 1891*

The CAUSE OF DEATH* was as follows: *Pneumonia, lobular*

7 AGE Years *27* | Months *5* | Days *24* | If LESS than 1 day, ... hrs. or ...... min.

(duration) ...... yrs. ...... mos. *5* ds.

CONTRIBUTORY (SECONDARY) *Influenza epidemic*

8 OCCUPATION OF DECEASED
(a) Trade, profession, or particular kind of work *Photographer*
(b) General nature of industry, business, or establishment in which employed (or employer) *Not Known*
(c) Name of employer

(duration) ...... yrs. ...... mos. *3* ds.

18 Where was disease contracted if not at place of death? ....

Did an operation precede death? *No* Date of ✓

9 BIRTHPLACE (city or town) *Ogden* (State or country) *Utah*

Was there an autopsy? *No*

What test confirmed diagnosis? ✓

10 NAME OF FATHER *Not Known*

(Signed) *Curtis Atkinson* major, M.C., M.D.

11 BIRTHPLACE OF FATHER (city or town) *Not Known* (State or country)

19 (Address) *Call Field, Wichita Falls Texas.*

12 MAIDEN NAME OF MOTHER *Not Known*

13 BIRTHPLACE OF MOTHER (city or town) *Not Known* (State or country)

* State the DISEASE CAUSING DEATH, or in deaths from VIOLENT CAUSES, state (1) MEANS AND NATURE OF INJURY, and (2) whether ACCIDENTAL, SUICIDAL, or HOMICIDAL. (See reverse side for additional space.)

14 Informant *C W Clark 14 H C.S. W*
(Address) *By A.W. Cud Lys. Ky. W*

19 PLACE OF BURIAL, CREMATION, OR REMOVAL *Ogden Utah* | **DATE OF BURIAL** 19

15 Filed *3 - 7*, 19*19* *M. A. Beckman* REGISTRAR

20 UNDERTAKER *A W Hines* *No Mills* | **ADDRESS**

Heber H. Thomas Death Certificate

Heber Harris Thomas was born May 12, 1891 in Ogden, Utah to Heber and Nellie Thomas. His father was a photographer running the Thomas Studio in Salt Lake City with his young son as his helper. Heber Jr. had married a young woman, Verlie Lambourne, with two small children, and soon after they had a son of their own, Raymond Harris Heber. Heber was a tall man, slender with dark brown hair and blue eyes.

One cannot but wonder if some of the pictures taken at Call Field were not the work of Heber Thomas, as that is listed as his occupation on his death certificate, and the field was home for the study of aerial photography.

Thomas fell ill to the beginning stages of Spanish Flu on October 9th and was sent to the post hospital. As with other cases, the symptoms escalated into pneumonia, and on October 17th, Heber Thomas died, another death attributed to pneumonia, lobular with influenza epidemic listed as the contributory factor.

Major Atkinson signed the death certificate like so many others, and the body was returned to Heber's native Utah, where he is buried in Salt Lake City.

The last death in October came the next day on October 18th. The young soldier was Benjamin Green Beach, or as everyone called him, Benny. Benny was born October 12, 1899 in Sadler, Texas in Grayson County.

His parents were Homer and Lula Richardson Beach. They were farmers, with Benny and his eight other siblings pitching in to do the work on the farm.

Benny came to Call Field in late July or early August and was a member of Squadron A at Call Field. Dr. Atkinson certified he had attended him at the hospital since October 9th. Benny suffered for nine days, finally surrendering to death on October 18th. Once more, the Major signed the certificate of death with the words, "pneumonia, lobular with the contributory factor, influenza."

Unlike all the others, Benny Beach was buried in this area at Burkburnett, Texas, just a few miles north of Wichita Falls.

A tombstone is in place today with the fitting words, "Benjamin Beach Oct. 12, 1899 –

Oct. 18, 1918. Early in the morning just in the bloom of life and love, and while in the service

of a righteous cause, he fell and hath gone before to greet us on the blissful shore."

Benjamin Beach Death Certificate

NOVEMBER

There was hope that since October finally ended, the death rate would diminish, but just because the name of the month changed does not mean that the epidemic was weakening its hold on the post.

November 22nd death claimed the life of another young cadet. William W. McBride was born November 1, 1894 to Thomas J. McBride and his wife, Roxanna in Ronda, North Carolina, but the family moved a few years later to Elwood, Indiana.

 William worked in a lumber yard until he enlisted into the army on December 15, 1917 in Indianapolis, Indiana. He was sent first to Columbus Barracks, Ohio, then was reassigned to Camp Grant, Illinois.

Upon completion of his training, he was sent to Aviation Mechanics Training School as a member of the 282nd Aero Squadron. After training there he was assigned to Call Field.

He was a popular cadet, well-liked by everyone, but as with so many others, he fell ill in mid-November and went into the post hospital on November 17th. He lingered from the symptoms of the Spanish Flu, and then as with the others pneumonia set in, and on November 22nd again Major Atkinson was filling out another death certificate of a dead soldier from Call Field. McBride's body was sent back home to Indiana, where was interred in the Elwood, Indiana Cemetery.

STANDARD CERTIFICATE OF DEATH

DEPARTMENT OF COMMERCE
BUREAU OF THE CENSUS

William McBride Death Certificate

The next day another casualty of the flu epidemic, Otto A. Petriet, fell victim and died.

Otto had been born January 24, 1890 in Waterbury, Connecticut to German parents, August

and August Petriet. He is listed on the 1900 census as Ador, but his name was probably

Americanized to Otto. He came to Call Field as a mechanic and had previously worked in

Connecticut as a toolmaker. He was 27 years old, stood 5'6½" tall and weighed 148 pounds,

according to his registration certificate.

On November 19th, the first effects of the flu hit Otto, and he went to the post hospital. He was cared for there until symptoms developed, as was the pattern, into pneumonia, which took his life at 9:55 a.m. on November 23rd. Dr. Curtis Atkinson was forced again to fill out yet another death certificate. As was the case in many of the other deaths, the local undertaker, O.W. Hines, prepared the body, but unlike many of the others, Otto Petriet remained here in Wichita Falls, buried at Riverside Cemetery.

Otto Petriet Death Certificate

Chester A. Chiles, '17, lieutenant in aviation corps. Died in Kansas November 29, 1918, of pneumonia following an attack of influenza.

They managed to get through Thanksgiving, 1918 without the grim reaper, but their luck played out on November 29th when another cadet died in the post hospital. His name was Chester Arthur Chiles. He had been born July 14, 1888 in San Luis, Colorado to Lincoln and Sarah Frances Searcy Chiles. On his registration card, he was listed as medium height and weight, and by the time he enlisted he was balding. He had worked previously for a mining company in Bisbie, Arizona, but was hoping to take up working with Boy Scouts after the war. His death certificate would list him as a school principal in Gleason, Arizona.

He had reached the status of Second Lieutenant at Call Field when he became ill on November 15th and entered the post hospital. He died there two weeks later of pneumonia, lobular with the influenza listed as a contributory factor. His body was sent to Ellensburg, Washington, where he was buried in the IOOF Cemetery.

With the end of November, many wondered what December would bring. They would shortly find out.

DECEMBER

George C. Hall Death Certificate

It only took until the first day of December for death to take another cadet's life. His name was George Clayton Hall, and he was from Monrovia, California, having been born in Bloomfield, Iowa, on either the 8th or 11th of September 1885 to Mr. and Mrs. E.C. Hall.

According to his registration card, he had worked prior to the war as a mechanic for a San Francisco traction company and was considered an expert in his field. He was tall and of medium build with blonde hair and blue eyes.

He was a little older than most but fit in well at Call Field .During the worst of the epidemic, George fell ill on November 20th and was placed in the post hospital. He died on December 1st at 4:45 p.m.

The Arcadia Tribute in Arcadia, California carried the following obituary:

"GIVEN MILITARY BURIAL…Body of the late George C. Hall was laid to rest in Live Oak Cemetery Saturday afternoon, while a circle of friends gathered around the grave where the body was being paid final military honors. A squad from the Army Battalion Sellout fired a round of shells, which bade adieu to all that was mortal of the young motor mechanic. The end had come. George Hall died at Call Field, Texas, December 2 (death certificate has December 1st) of pneumonia. He, Hall, 125 East Orange Avenue, was the son of Mr. and Mrs. E.C. Hall of Monrovia. The young man enlisted at San Francisco and was assigned to the 'aviation field in Texas.' He won the admiration of his fellow soldiers, and when death occurred and his body brought back to Monrovia for burial, Major James Alfonte wired his parents an appreciation of his services. The funeral services were conducted by Dr. Charles Coke Woods, pastor of the Methodist Church. He paid a beautiful tribute to the memory of the young man, who had given his life in training camp while in preparation for participation in the great battle for world peace."

After Hall's death, there was a quiet lull of a couple of weeks before the last victim of the Spanish Flu epidemic succumbed.

The cadet was a young man names Ernest B. Arnold. He had been born on August 24, 1892 in Hudson, New Jersey to Willie and Mary Bergen Arnold. According to the 1900 census for Hoboken, New Jersey, Ernest lived with his parents and two brothers. By 1917 another brother was added to the family.

On June 5, 1917 Ernest registered for the draft at the age of 24. At the time he was teaching Industrial Education for the State of New Jersey. His registration card describes him as tall, slender, with brown hair and brown eyes. He was assigned to Call Field in the 192nd Aero Squadron and arrived at Call Field that same year.

He fell ill with the flu on December 9th and fought for his life until losing it on December 16th shortly before 8:00 a.m.

Atkinson signed another death certificate with the familiar notation, pneumonia, lobular, contributory factor, influenza.

Arnold's body was shipped back to his beloved New Jersey, where he is interred in the Holy Name Cemetery in Jersey City, New Jersey, another young man who had come so far, only to die.

Cadet Almon Lincoln, flying one of Call Field's planes, 1918.

Armistice Day, November 12, 1918 was the day all hostilities were to cease. World War I was over, but the pilots still trained at the air fields, and Call Field was no different.

That routine training resulted in a horrific airplane crash and the deaths of two more young men. Lieutenant Clarence E. Holburn and cadet A.K. Lincoln were killed in the crash

Clarence E. Holburn of Brooklyn, New York was the younger son of Mrs. M.E. Hand Holburn, who owned the Hotel Delavan and Holburn Hall in Sayville, New York. Clarence had been born in Bayonne, New Jersey, but for most of his young life lived in Brooklyn. When war was declared, he promptly enlisted in the Aviation Corps and went to Cornell University for instruction, then on to Mineola where he received his commission.

Before his enlistment, he was employed as an advertising man by the Hyatt Roller Bearing Company. Clarence was tall, of medium build, with brown eyes and brown hair.

Newspaper accounts of his obituary focused on his character and potentially bright future. One said, "Lieutenant Holburn, who was a very bright young man, left an excellent position to study the science of aviation at the Cornell Ground School. After finishing there, he was stationed for a time at Mineola, and on several occasions made landings on the field on the North Country Road here used by Mineola aviators. His superior officers frankly said that he was a very clever student and seemed to be a born flyer.

The telegram telling of his death came to his home on Tuesday, and the message had to be taken to his mother where she was at work in one of Brooklyn's Red Cross branches in which organization Mrs. Holburn has been very active."

Another newspaper said, "Lt. Holburn was born in Bayonne, New Jersey, 24 years old, and he and his brother, Walter F., were brought up at Sayville, Long Island, where the interment will take place Sunday, preceded by a military funeral in which a guard of honor and pallbearers will be furnished with the Mineola Flying Field authorities. The services this evening will be at his mother's home, 108 Linden Avenue, the Reverend C.C. Albertson of the Lafayette Avenue Presbyterian Church officiating. The religious services will be followed by a Masonic service conducted by the officers of the Acanhus Lodge No. 719 of which Lt. Holburn was a member. He was also a member of the Aero Club of America."

Holburn-Lincoln Crash

The other man killed in the accident was probably one of the most well-liked and popular cadets at the field. His name was Almon Kemp Lincoln and was born in Worchester, Massachusetts, September 30, 1895 to Edwin Hale and Hattie Kemp Lincoln. The parents were residents of Dalton, Massachusetts, but after a few months moved to Pittsfield, which they called home. Almon graduated from high school in1914 and then entered North Carolina State College the next year, leaving there before his freshman year was over and enrolling in Worcester Polytechnic Institute. He was elected president of his class.

On February 21, 1918, he enlisted into the Signal Corps of the United States Army, Division of Military Aeronautics but was allowed to finish his sophomore year before being called into service on May 28th.

He was first sent to Princeton University for study and instruction in ground work. He completed that instruction and was then sent to Dallas, Texas to Camp Dick, then on to Call Field for instruction in flying.

Within a letter to Almon's parents from the Commandant of Cadets, 1st Lieut. Galen Horner gives us the most vivid details of the accident that killed two pilots.

"As immediate commanding officer of your son, the late Almon K. Lincoln, I want to extend to you my heartfelt sympathy in this time of bereavement."

"Your son was taking flying instructions with one of the cleanest and most noble of our flying instructors. On this morning of December 3rd, when coming into the field to land my ship, I saw at a distance a ship seemingly out of control. First it went into what is termed a stall, then it fell off to one side and started into what is called a tailspin. At this time, I became very uneasy as they were then so near the ground. Lieutenant Holburn at this moment kicked it out of the spin, and the ship then started straight for the ground, nose foremost. As a result of this crash, your son met instant death." (Another newspaper account said he lived a few seconds after they got to the plane, but that he had a broken neck. It stated Holburn had "every bone in his body broken."

Horner goes on to say, "I want to inform you that the loss of your son and Lieutenant Holburn have been more keenly felt than any other fatality we have ever had on this post, both by the enlisted men, cadets, and officers. He has died in the full execution of his duty, and by making this supreme sacrifice as much honor is due him as any of the boys who were killed in action across the seas. Your son stood very high in the esteem of his fellow cadets and among the officers immediately over him."

Almon K. Lincoln

He went on to say if he had lived another week, he would have chosen him to be the 1st

Assistant to the Chief Cadet Section Marcher, which was a distinction of achievement and

ability.

A newspaper account tells of how 12 airplanes from Call Field flew for over an hour on either

side of the train as it returned the body to Massachusetts. It was as if they refused to let him

go. The service for A.K. Lincoln was held at the Clapp Mortuary Chapel at 2:00 p.m. on a

Saturday. The Reverend Payson Pierce performed the service, and at the grave site a firing

squad from Company K of the state guard carried out military honors. Taps was sounded

over the casket, which was draped with an American flag.

THE LAST MAN

In April of 1973, a young soldier, John Kerry, speaking for the Vietnam Veterans Against the War, asked the famous question of the Senate Committee on Foreign Relations, "How do you ask a man to be the last man to die in Vietnam?"

Kerry went on to become a U.S. Senator, a Presidential candidate for the Democratic Party, and Secretary of State during the second half of the 8 year Obama Administration, but aside from all of his achievements, he is most remembered for the haunting question of who do you ask to die last for any cause?

Edward Martin Andersen was that man for Call Field.

Edward Andersen was born March 1, 1895 in New York to John Martin and Laura Petrea Jensen Andersen, both of whose parents had been born in Denmark, hence the spelling of the surname as Andersen, instead of the English spelling, Anderson. (Regretfully, his name is misspelled on the Call Field Memorial Monument.) Edward's father, John, died in 1905 at the age of 35.

The war was over and Joseph Kemp, who had been a force in getting Cal Field started, was delegated by Wichita Falls city fathers to go to Washington DC to try and convince military officials to keep the post open as a permanent training facility. For some reason, Kemp decided that it was not a good time to push for such an action and did not go.

Lacking extra support, Call Field, like other military bases after the war, was closed to cut unnecessary defense spending. The inventory was sent to other air fields and bases.

Edward Andersen was tasked with the job of flying an airplane to Love Field in Dallas for storage there. The Galveston Daily News account of Saturday, July 26, 1919 gives us the most accurate account of what happened.

"AVIATOR IS KILLED IN FALL AT LOVE FIELD DALLAS, TEXAS, JULY 25 --- Second Lieutenant Edward M. Andersen, from Call Field, Wichita Falls, Texas was instantly killed when his plane fell as he was preparing to land at Love Field at 3:30 o'clock this afternoon. Lieutenant Andersen was bringing from Call Field to Love Field for storage a Curtis-JN-4-plane. At an elevation of 100 feet, his right wing partly collapsed, which caused his plane to take a nose dive. Edward was killed when his Curtiss Jenny crashed on approach to Love Field in Dallas, Texas."

Edward's remains were sent to Richmond Hill, New York, where he was interred; the last man from Call Field to die.

LOST IN TIME

If there are actually footnotes to history, there are some whose names belong here.

<table>
<tr><td colspan="5">Cardwell, Mary B</td><td>OFFICER—ORC
white</td></tr>
<tr><td>(Surname)</td><td></td><td>(Christian name)</td><td></td><td></td><td></td></tr>
</table>

```
                                        Cardwell,      Mary B                    OFFICER—ORC
                                                                                    white
            (Surname)                    (Christian name)

Residence........... 200 E 16 St.,    Austin,    Travis— TEXAS
            (Street and house number)    (Town or city)    (County)    (State)

* Born in              Buda, Texas   Oct 25/81
† Called into active service as   Nurse Sept 11/18 fr CL          ‡ XXX Training Camp.
  Promotions :         none

  Organizations and
  staff assignments :  Post Hosp Call Field Texas to disch

  Principal
  XXXXXXX

  Engagements :        none

  Wounds received in action : None.
  § Served overseas    none      Relieved physically unfit
  ‖ Hon. disch.        Oct 3/18   XXXXXXXXXXXXXXXXXXXXXXXXXXXXXXXXX
  Was reported         XX    per cent disabled on date of discharge, in view of occupation.
  Remarks :

Form No. 84c–1      * Give place and date.  † Insert (a) grade ; (b) arm or staff corps or department ; (c) date ;
  A. G. O.          (d) source, civil life (CL), RA, NG, ORC, NA ; and (e) designation of training camp attended, if
  Mar. 17, 1921.    any.  ‡ Strike out if he did not attend a training camp.  § Give dates of departure from and return
                    to the United States.  ‖ Give date.                                    3—8091
```

The first was a woman, Marie Cardwell. Mary/Marie B. Cardwell was born October 25, 1881 in Buda, Hays County Texas. She was the daughter of John Nelson and Alice Turner Cardwell. Marie became a nurse and was a member of the Travis County Registered Nurses Association. She enlisted from Austin, Texas in the service of the government under the American Red Cross.

Cardwell was called to duty September 11, 1918 and was assigned to Call Field to assist at the post hospital with the many flu cases. She served at the post hospital for two weeks before falling ill herself. After contracting the flu, she was sent to San Antonio, Texas for treatment. She died on October 4th.

The death certificate provides an even more tragic picture as it states she died in San Antonio, Texas, having been there for two weeks before her death, a death that was caused by exhaustion, but the contributory factor is listed as manic-depressive insanity.

She was buried in Live Oak Cemetery in Manchaca, Texas, SW section, row 5, grave 13.

Marie Cardwell had passed through the gates of Call Field only long enough to become exposed to its deadly epidemic, then die. An Austin, Texas, newspaper account stated that "She gave her life in the hour of her country's need, nursing the soldiers in the terrible epidemic scourge."

The second name is 1st Lieutenant Ralph Koontz. Ralph was born in Saint Louisville, Ohio, August 7, 1892 to Franklin and Emma Price Koontz. According to the 1920 census, he was living in Newton, Licking County, Ohio and was employed as a public school teacher. His occupation listed on his draft registration card (1917) was farming, being employed by his father.

Koontz was commissioned at Fort Benjamin Harrison in 1917 and was a part of the Signal Corps, having attended training school at Signal Corps Radio School, College Park, Maryland. Koontz was not stationed at Call Field. He was in fact a radio officer at Henry Post Field in Lawton, Oklahoma.

On a Tuesday, April 22nd about 3:30 p.m., Koontz was with a party doing cross country work when his plane went into a side slip as he was leaving Call Field, and he fell about 200 feet to his death. Lieutenant Koontz' body was returned to Newark, Ohio, where he was buried in the Wilson Cemetery.

The last two were Dr. Curtis Atkinson and his wife, Mary Ann Monroe Atkinson. Major Atkinson was the attending doctor who signed nearly all the death certificates for the casualties at Call Field. He had been born in Benton County, Indiana in 1874. His wife, Mary Ann, was born in 1899 in Memphis, Missouri.

Dr. Atkinson died in 1957 when he was 82 and is buried in Wichita Falls at Riverside Cemetery. His wife died in 1998 at the age of 99 and is buried next to her husband. Their only child, Grame Lindsey Atkinson, died in 1948.

THE MONUMENT REMAINS

HAROLD IMBRIE DIED 4-24-18 1ST LT
B. JACKSON JR. DIED 4-1-18 2ND LT
S.R. WARNER DIED 4-24-18 2ND LT
H.S. ROSS DIED 7-11-18 2ND LT
F.R. McGIFFIN DIED 8-30-18 2ND LT
C.A. CHILES DIED 11-29-18 2ND LT
C.E. HOLBURN DIED 12-3-18 2ND LT
E.M. ANDERSON DIED 7-25-19 2ND LT
P.T. WHITTLE DIED 10-12-18 CORP.
O.A. PETRIE T DIED 11-23-18 CHAUF. 1ST CL
E.B. ARNOLD DIED 12-16-18 CHAUF.
H.P. GAME DIED 2-8-18 PVT. 1ST CL
J.R. DES CHAMPS DIED 3-21-18 PVT. 1ST CL
O.G. FRANKS DIED 3-27-18 PVT. 1ST CL
E.D. CRYER DIED 4-24-18 PVT. 1ST CL
J.T. VAN AUKEN DIED 5-18-18 PVT. 1ST CL
E.R. BABCOCK DIED 8-30-18 PVT. 1ST CL
A.K. LINCOLN DIED 12-3-18 PVT. 1ST CL
T.H. JAMES DIED 2-10-18 PVT.
C.L. STEVENS DIED 5-1-18 PVT.
W.H. LEES DIED 7-4-18 PVT.
C. WILLIAMS DIED 10-13-18 PVT.
E.V. RHODES DIED 10-14-18 PVT.
R. FARREN JR. DIED 10-16-18 PVT.
H.H. THOMAS DIED 10-17-18 PVT.
B.G. BEACH DIED 30-18-18 PVT.
W. McBRIDE DIED 11-22-18 PVT.
G.C. HALE DIED 12-1-18 PVT.

So now after 100 years we have put the pieces of the puzzle back together. The Call Field Memorial Monument can be seen today at the entrance to the Wichita Falls Regional Airport Terminal.

According to a newspaper article from Sunday, October 31, 1937, the Wichita Falls Junior Chamber of Commerce (Jaycees) and the Pat Carrigan American Legion Post cooperated to erect the marker at then Lake Road and Call Field.

At some point, probably due to construction and city growth, the marker was moved to the area between what is now Cunningham Elementary School and the Boys and Girls Club.

It remained a silent witness to the existence of the field until the 21st century arrived and the Museum of North Texas History, spearheaded by board member Robert Seabury and financed through numerous private and public sources, bought a restored Curtiss Jenny plane and was able to develop a Call Field Museum near Kickapoo Airport on the Jacksboro Highway. The plane was flown once a month when the weather permitted, but when plans fell into place for the City of Wichita Falls to build a new airport, it seemed like the final flight needed to be taken. The plane was landed for the last time inside the airport building, surrounded by artifacts, an automobile, uniforms, media players, dioramas, and a stunning mural of life at Call Field.

The monument was placed outside the visitors' entrance to the airport and included the names of those who died at Call Field. It only included last names, except for one, all others using initials. Research volunteers from the North Texas Genealogical Association tracked down the complete names of the young men plus their military records, death certificates, and obituaries when available.

The attempt to identify and clarify the names on this beautiful granite monument was done out of respect for their contributions to our country, a sense of history, and to show honor to those who gave their all for this nation.

We all want to be remembered and for others to remember our loved ones. So now, using that as a point of reference, may we realize as we view this monument, or others like it, that it is more than just a name that we honor, but a life, although extinguished too soon, given in service to our great nation.

REFERENCES

1. Tuttle, Dwight, "Wichita Heritage Magazine," 1991

2. Ibid

3. Ibid

4. Galbraith, Laura, &

5. Hadwai, Joseph, "Wichita Falls at War, the Great War on the Homefront.

Ancestry.com

Newspapers online

Wichita County Archives

ABOUT THE AUTHOR

Kenny Mayo is a retired educator and member of the board at the Museum of North Texas History. He taught history for 33 years at City View I.S.D. along with coaching duties. He has written three previous books, *"Would You Like Mayo with That?"*, *"The Golden Age of the Honky-Tonk,"* and *"I'm Not a Preacher...But if I Was, This is What I Would Say."* He and his wife, Susan, are the parents of two daughters, Mandy Story and Marly Smith, and grandparents of four grandsons, Robby and Jacob Story and Jaxon and Brody Smith. The Mayo's are musicians who perform with their band, "Post Oak," for programs at the museum, as well as for churches, presentations for clubs, and various other functions.

Made in the USA
Coppell, TX
28 October 2020